BIBLE LEARNING GAMES

Grades 3 & 4

Mary Rose Pearson

These pages may be copied.

Rainbow Publishers

Rainbow Publishers • P.O. Box 261129 • San Diego, CA 92196
www.rainbowpublishers.com

*To the thousands of children who have attended my kids' crusades and who
call me Aunt Mary.*

Mary Rose Pearson

"O God, Thou hast taught me from my youth: and hitherto have I
declared Thy wondrous works. Now also when I am old and grayheaded,
O God, forsake me not; until I have shown Thy strength unto this genera-
tion, and Thy power to every one that is to come."
— *Psalm 71:17-18*

Bible Learning Games: Grades 3&4
©2003 by Rainbow Publishers, ninth printing
ISBN 0-937282-75-8
Rainbow reorder# RB36254
church and ministry/ministry resources/children's ministry

Rainbow Publishers
P.O. Box 261129
San Diego, CA 92196
www.rainbowpublishers.com

Illustrator: Fran Kizer

Unless otherwise indicated, all Scripture is taken from the King James Version of the Bible.

Scripture marked NIV is from the *Holy Bible: New International Version* (North American
Edition), ©1973, 1978, 1984 by the International Bible Society. Used by permission of
Zondervan Bible Publishers.

Printed in the United States of America

INTRODUCTION

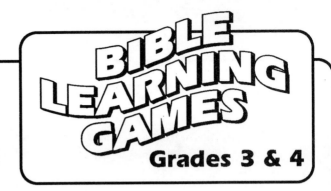

These *Bible Learning Games* teach positive values as well as cooperation, patience, friendship, and kindness. As they play, children absorb Bible truths, improve mental and physical skills, and learn to interact with other children and adults.

Games are a valuable teaching tool. They bring variety, fun, and a change of pace to the classroom. More important, they are not simply time fillers or "play" after the real "work" has been done. These Bible games effectively teach the Word of God. Each game includes a Bible memory verse which can be memorized during the game to help children learn God's word.

These games and activities may be used in Sunday school, Vacation Bible School, children's church, Bible clubs, or wherever the Bible is being taught. Because third and fourth grade children love doing familiar things — singing the same songs, hearing the same stories, and playing the same games again and again — these games may be used over and over. You may tire of the repetition, but they won't!

Every game is easy to learn, requires minimal preparation time, and comes with complete instructions and illustrations to ensure immediate success. If "props" are required, ordinary household materials are suggested. Multiple copies of instructions and patterns may be duplicated from this book for classroom use.

As with all activities, children's safety should be a top priority; children should be closely supervised at all times. A child with a broken leg, in a wheelchair, or with other special needs, should be included in all of the games by pairing him with an older child or an adult to assist him, if necessary. When the game requires movement, position that child at the goal line to help arbitrate close calls, or have him hold the tape recorder and push the button to stop or start the music.

These *Bible Learning Games* encompass a wide variety of both quiet and active games and activities, which are divided into the following sections:

Circle Games involve the entire group playing together as they learn Bible stories and concepts. If you have a very large group, divide the children into two teams, and have them play simultaneously.

Move-About Games give third and fourth grade children the opportunity to use some of their energy in creative play, while learning Bible facts and memory verses. These games also teach children how to play safely and fairly.

Bible stories and facts are reinforced when children play **Bible Knowledge Games.** A variety of drills, quizzes, and games capture children's interest as they review important people and events of the Bible. Quizzes and patterns can be photocopied and used year after year.

When children sing Bible truths, they remember them. And they will enjoy singing the easy to learn songs and playing the **Sing-A-Long Games.** Music is included for each song.

Paper & Pencil Games require less physical activity but will stimulate children mentally as they learn to recognize the names of Bible characters, discover ways to be a good example, and begin learning about God's plan of salvation.

Relays & Races require a team effort to be successful. These games develop muscle coordination, Bible knowledge, spelling and geography skills, and teach children to cooperate and work together.

All of these games and activities — over 40 in all — will bring new fun, excitement, and spiritual learning to any classroom of third and fourth grade children.

TABLE OF CONTENTS

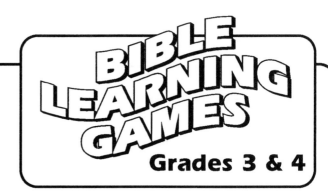

BIBLE LEARNING GAMES
Grades 3 & 4

INDEX

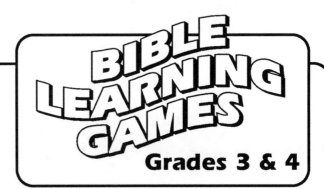

BIBLE LEARNING GAMES

Grades 3 & 4

Old Grouch

This game helps children learn that true happiness comes from God.

MEMORY VERSE

"Rejoice in the Lord always: and again I say, Rejoice." — Philippians 4:4

PREPARATION

Duplicate one sheet of game cards from page 8 for each player. Provide crayons, scissors, glue, poster board for the back of each sheet, and clear adhesive-backed plastic for both sides.

HOW TO PLAY

1. Give each child a game card sheet and crayons. Have children color their game sheet, cover the back with glue, and attach it to a piece of poster board. Help them cover both sides of the game cards with clear, adhesive-backed plastic. (An adult should supervise this closely.) They may then cut the cards apart. Provide a table or floor area for each team.
2. Plan to have no more than 6 or 8 players per team, so play several games simultaneously, if necessary. Each team should have one set of cards (9 cards) per player, with only one Old Grouch card per team.
3. Read the verses on the cards aloud before playing the game. Discuss any that may be confusing. Point out the Old Grouch card, and ask the children to explain his verse.

4. The players sit in a circle on the floor or at a table. Choose a dealer to shuffle the cards and pass them out one at a time, around the circle, until all the cards have been dealt. The players hold their cards in their hands so that the others cannot see them. If a player has a pair (two cards whose verses match), he places both cards in front of him on the table or floor.
5. Then, taking turns, each player draws a card from the player to his left, always putting down any pairs with each play. The object is to see who can get the most pairs (the winner) and who will be left holding the Old Grouch (the loser). If time allows, it will be helpful to review and discuss the verses on the cards once again after playing the game.

The righteous
doth sing
and rejoice.
(Proverbs 29:6)

The joy
of the Lord
is your strength.
(Nehemiah 8:10)

I will joy in the
God of my
salvation.
(Habakkuk 3:18)

Happy is he . . .
whose hope is in
the Lord his God.
(Psalm 146:5)

Rejoice, because
your names are
written in heaven.
(Luke 10:20)

The fruit of the
Spirit is love,
joy, peace.
(Galatians 5:22)

My soul shall be
joyful in my God.
(Isaiah 61:10)

In Thy presence
is fulness of joy.
(Psalm 16:11)

Whoso trusteth
in the Lord,
happy is he.
(Proverbs 16:20)

Many sorrows
shall be to
the wicked.
(Psalm 32:10)

Who's the Leader?

This game reminds children that others are watching them, so they should always be good examples.

MEMORY VERSE

"Don't let anyone look down on you because you are young, but set an example for the believers."
— I Timothy 4:12 (NIV)

PREPARATION

If chairs are used, arrange them in a circle with an open area for It to enter and leave the circle. You will need one chair for each player except It.

HOW TO PLAY

1. Choose someone to be It. All other players are seated in a circle in chairs or on the floor. It leaves the room and a leader is chosen, who begins to clap. Everyone quickly follows his example.
2. Clapping is the signal for It to reenter the room and stand in the center of the circle. When the leader thinks It is not looking at him, he begins snapping, patting his head or knees, shuffling his feet, etc. The other players, while trying not to look directly at him, do whatever the leader does.
3. It has three guesses to name the leader. If he guesses correctly, the leader becomes It. If he fails to identify the leader, he is It another time. After two or three rounds of guessing incorrectly, a new player is chosen to be It. The former It takes that seat, and the game continues until each child has had a turn to be the leader.

TO TALK ABOUT

What actions can you do that would be good examples to others? What actions would be bad examples? Whose help must you have in order to be a good example?

Capture the Philistines

WE CAUGHT A PHILISTINE!

This game helps children learn that the only way to defeat spiritual enemies is to trust and obey God.

MEMORY VERSE

"Be not afraid . . . for the battle is not yours, but God's." — II Chronicles 20:15

PREPARATION

Bring a tape player and a music cassette tape or invite someone to play the piano or guitar (or have the leader clap). Provide a large area, away from chairs and tables, for this game.

HOW TO PLAY

1. Divide the players into two teams, the Israelites and the Philistines. Decide how many times you will play the game — perhaps five or seven. The winner of the most rounds wins the game.
2. The Israelites form a large circle while holding hands, which they lift high. The Philistines form a circle outside, around the Israelites, but do not clasp hands.
3. As music is played or clapping begins, the Philistines march around the circle, weaving in and out, under the hands of the Israelites. When the music or clapping stops, the Israelites must quickly lower their hands. The Philistines who are left inside the circle have been captured and must leave the game.
4. The Israelites raise their hands again as music is played or clapping begins, and the game continues for as many rounds as were pre-selected. Count the number of Philistines captured and those still in the game. If a larger number have been captured, the Israelites win. If there are more Philistines still in the game, the Philistines win.
5. If time allows, play five rounds, then switch places. (The Israelites become Philistines and move to the outside circle, and the Philistines become Israelites.) Play another five rounds in this new position.

TO TALK ABOUT

Explain that the Israelites won and lost many battles with their enemies. They always won if they were serving and obeying God, but they lost when they disobeyed Him and worshiped idols (Joshua 23:10-13). Discuss ways this applies to the children as they face temptations and troubles in their own lives.

Old or New Testament?

This game helps children learn which books of the Bible are in the Old Testament and which are in the New Testament.

MEMORY VERSE

"From a child thou hast known the Holy Scriptures."
— II Timothy 3:15

PREPARATION

Print on two 3 x 5-inch (or 4 x 6-inch) cards the words OLD and NEW, one word per card. Glue the cards onto two shoe boxes. Print each of the first ten books of the Old and New Testaments on 3 x 5-inch cards, one book per card. Tape a large X on the floor. Bring a tape player and music cassette or invite someone to play the piano or guitar (or have the leader clap).

HOW TO PLAY

1. Before playing the game, teach the children the books of the Bible so that they can read them and tell whether they are from the Old or New Testament. Place the two boxes on a table near the playing area. Lay the cards face down in a pile beside them. Have the children practice before the game, taking turns choosing a card and placing it in the correct box.
2. Have the children stand in a circle which includes the X. Count off by ones and twos to form two teams. (Both teams remain in the circle.) An adult leader should stand near the table with a score sheet. If possible, the score sheet should be on an easel or posted so all players can see it.
3. As the music plays or leader claps, the players march in a circle. When the music or clapping stops, the player standing nearest the X must go to the table, draw a card from the pile, and place it in the correct box. If he places it correctly, his team gets 100 points. If incorrectly, his team gets no points. The child then returns to the circle, and the game continues. The team with the highest score wins.
4. With a very young group, begin playing with fewer Bible book names. Keep adding names until the children learn all the Bible books.

Holy Land Journey

I AM GOING WITH JOHN, PAUL AND MARK.

This game helps children learn the names of Bible characters and whether they are located in the Old or New Testament.

MEMORY VERSE

"These all . . . obtained a good report through faith."
— Hebrews 11:39

PREPARATION

If chairs are used, arrange them in a circle, one for each child.

HOW TO PLAY

1. Discuss various men and women of the Bible before playing this game. Ask children to name the Bible story or book of the Bible each person is from. Have them describe one or two things each person did (denied Jesus three times, asked for healing, parted the Red Sea, helped her mother-in-law after her husband and sons died, collected taxes, etc.).

2. Seat the players in a circle. State whether the Bible characters to be named will be men or women. Choose a player to begin. He will say, "I am taking a journey through the Holy Land. I am going with _____ (naming a Bible character in the category of men or women)." The next player says the same thing and adds a character.

3. Continue, with each player naming all the characters that have been given and adding one. If a person fails to give all the names or gives one not in the category, he is out of the game and must remain silent as the others continue. If you wish, after all have played, go back around again without adding names to see how many can name all the Bible characters mentioned during the game.

ANOTHER WAY TO PLAY

1. When the children can name many characters, have them name the characters, not only by gender, but also by whether they're in the Old or New Testament. Play as above, but have the first player say, "I am taking an Old Testament Journey through the Holy Land. I am going with _____ (naming a person in the Old Testament)."

2. Continue, with each player naming all the previous characters and adding one more. If a person fails to give all the names or gives one not in the category, he is out of the game.

Saul and David

This game reviews the story of David's flight from Saul (I Samuel 22-24) and David's trust in God (Psalm 57).

MEMORY VERSE

"Be merciful unto me, O God . . . in the shadow of Thy wings will I make my refuge." — Psalm 57:1

PREPARATION

You will need two bean bags or balls of different colors. This game requires the same number of players on each team.

HOW TO PLAY

1. The players stand in a circle and count off by ones and twos to divide into two teams. Give a player on Team One a bean bag or ball (Saul). Across the circle from him, give a player on Team Two the other bean bag or ball (David). Team One tries to help Saul catch David, and Team Two tries to help David escape.
2. Give a signal for passing the bean bags. Team members pass the bags to members of their own team. A player with the bag reaches across the opposing team member standing beside him to pass the bag to his closest teammate.
3. A player holding the Saul bean bag catches David by tagging the player to his immediate left or right when that player is holding the David bean bag. Team One may change Saul's direction at any time. Team Two players must be alert and change David's direction also. The game is over when Saul catches David.

TO TALK ABOUT

Even though David was finally caught in the game, we know Saul, in the Bible story, never caught David. David made God his refuge, and God protected him. We should make God our refuge, too. Discuss things we can do to make God our refuge.

Stormy Galilee

This game helps children become familiar with the names of the disciples and the story of Jesus walking on water.

MEMORY VERSE

"Be of good cheer: it is I; be not afraid."
— Mark 6:50

PREPARATION

Arrange chairs in a row, one behind the other. Provide a chair for each player except It. The row of chairs will be the disciples' boat.

HOW TO PLAY

1. Choose one child to be It (Jesus). If the children have not yet learned the names of the disciples, give each of the other children the name of a disciple. If you have more than 12 players, give two players the same name. With fewer players, leave out some names.
2. If the children have already been studying the names of the disciples, provide a quick review. Have them take turns naming a disciple, until all 12 have been named. If you have more than 12 players, have them continue, naming each of the disciples once more, until each child has named a disciple.
3. The disciples sit in the chairs. It circles the boat, calling out any names he chooses, and those players must get up and follow him. When he calls out, "Stormy Galilee," everyone, including It, tries to sit in a chair. The one left out becomes the next It. Continue playing until most children have had a turn to be It.

TO TALK ABOUT

As soon as Jesus stepped into the boat, the storm stopped. When we let Him take control of our life, He will help us when the bad times come. That doesn't mean that the bad times will disappear completely. But Jesus has the power to calm the storms in our lives and to help us get through the bad times.

Pass the Cards

This game teaches children about the miracles in the Bible. It can also be used to review memory verses.

MEMORY VERSE

"Thy word is true from the beginning."
— Psalm 119:160

PREPARATION

Duplicate the Bible Miracles quiz from page 60. You will need as many quiz questions as there are players. Write the numbers of the quiz questions on index cards, one number per card. (Prepare more than enough, and simply omit those that are not needed.) On a few cards, draw or glue a gold star. Provide an empty box for each team, and label them TEAM 1 and TEAM 2.

HOW TO PLAY

1. Have the players stand in a circle. Divide into two teams by counting off in ones and twos. Place the two boxes in the center of the circle and give each player a card. The leader holds the quiz questions and a pencil. At the leader's signal, the players begin to pass the cards around to the right.
2. When the leader calls, "Stop," players stop passing the cards. The leader reads the #1 quiz question aloud, and the person holding the #1 card must answer it. If he answers correctly, he places that card in his team's box. (It may be helpful for the leader to place a check by that

quiz question as a reminder that the card is no longer in the game.) If he answers incorrectly, the card stays in the game.
3. Continue, calling for the numbers in consecutive order. After #20, return to #1 and continue calling for any cards still in the game. When all the cards have been put in the boxes, count them. A team receives 100 points for each card, and 500 points for a card with a gold star.

OTHER WAYS TO PLAY

1. This game may be used to teach other Bible concepts. Use one of the other quizzes from pages 61-64, and play as above with the numbered cards.
2. This game may also be used to reinforce memory verses. Write the Scripture references as well as the numbers on the cards. The person with #1 will say the verse called for on his card, etc.

MOVE-ABOUT GAMES

Red Light

This game demonstrates that God has given us rules (red lights) to obey which warn us to stop and think before acting.

MEMORY VERSE

"Direct my footsteps according to Your Word." — Psalm 119:133 (NIV)

PREPARATION

Mark a home base line about two feet from one end of the room (or outdoors) with masking tape or chalk. At least twelve feet away, if possible, mark another line (the goal line).

HOW TO PLAY

1. Before playing this game for the first time, explain that you will be playing a version of "Red Light, Green Light." Have one of the children describe how it is played. Explain that in the Bible God gives rules for Christians to live by. Some rules tell what we should do and some tell us what we shouldn't do. These rules are like red lights, telling us to stop and think before we act. Explain that when we are tempted to do wrong things or not to do right things, we should say, "Red Light," to ourselves. Then we should do what God's Book tells us to do.

2. Let the children look up and read these rules: (You may have additional rules to add to these lists.)

DO
Obey parents. (Colossians 3:20)
Go to church. (Hebrews 10:25)
Read the Bible. (Psalm 119:16)
Love your enemies. (Matthew 5:44)

DON'T
Lie. (Colossians 3:9)
Steal. (Exodus 20:15)
Love Money. (I Timothy 6:10)
Curse. (Exodus 20:7)

3. Choose one player to be It. He stands behind the goal line. The other players stand behind the other line (home base). It turns his back and starts counting. The others start running toward the opposite line as soon as It begins counting.

4. When It counts as many numbers as he wishes, he calls, "Red Light!" All players must stop immediately, and stand still. It turns around on the word "Light," and names any players he sees moving. Each of these must name a rule in the Bible which God gave to Christians.

5. If a player cannot name a rule, he must return to the home base line and begin again. A player may not repeat a rule which has already been given during that round. The player who reaches the goal line and returns back to home base first is the winner. He becomes It for the next game.

Find the Match

WE'RE A MATCH!

This game helps children remember Bible stories by matching Bible characters with objects that had significance in their lives.

MEMORY VERSE

"Thus you will walk in the ways of good men and keep to the paths of the righteous."
— Proverbs 2:20 (NIV)

PREPARATION

Duplicate the pictures from page 18 and the names below. Cut them apart and glue them to 3 x 5-inch cards, one picture or group of names per card (18 total cards). Laminate the cards or cover them with clear, adhesive-backed plastic.

HOW TO PLAY

1. You will need pairs of cards based on the number of players, one pair for every two players. Give each player a name or an object card, face down. If you have an odd number of players, take a card for yourself, too. At your signal, each player turns his card over and holds it in front of him as he searches for the person holding the object that goes with his character (or vice versa).

2. When a couple thinks they have a match, they must come to a leader for confirmation. Have them explain how their character used the object. The first couple to correctly match their name and object wins.

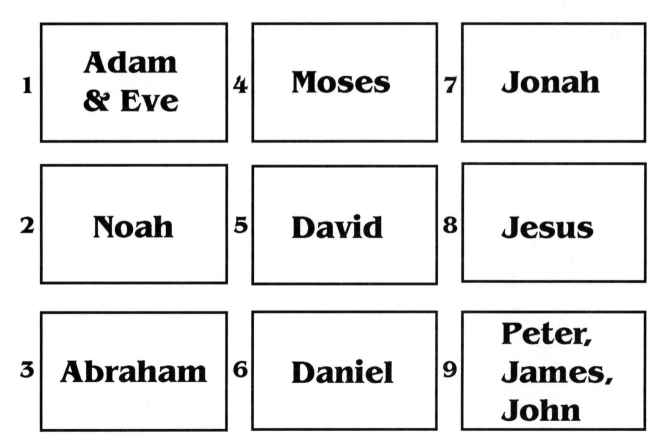

1 Adam & Eve	**4** Moses	**7** Jonah
2 Noah	**5** David	**8** Jesus
3 Abraham	**6** Daniel	**9** Peter, James, John

1

2

3

4

5

6

7

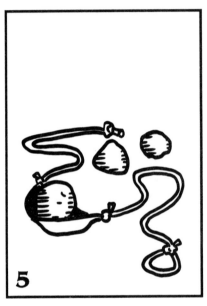

8

9

True-False Jumps

This game helps children understand that the Bible is God's Word.

MEMORY VERSE

"Because I consider all Your precepts right, I hate every wrong path." — Psalm 119:128 (NIV)

PREPARATION

With chalk or masking tape mark off two parallel lines across the room or outside, about 18 inches apart. You will need a copy of the True-False Quiz from page 61.

HOW TO PLAY

1. Designate one line True and the other False, and have the players stand between them. Read a statement from the quiz. Players must jump over either the True or the False line. No changing sides after the jump!
2. Have players explain why they jumped to one side or the other. Discuss the answers. Continue playing until all the statements have been read.

TO TALK ABOUT

Where do we find God's statements? What can we do to show we believe what the Bible says?

Split Verses

This game helps children memorize Bible verses and their Scripture references.

MEMORY VERSE

"Your words . . . were my joy and my heart's delight." — Jeremiah 15:16 (NIV)

PREPARATION

Select several memory verses, one for every two children. Write the Scripture reference on a slip of paper, and write the verse on another, one reference or verse per paper.

HOW TO PLAY

1. Give each player a memory verse slip to read silently. At your signal, they must find the person with the matching reference or verse by calling out the information on their slip.
2. The first couple with a correct match gets 100 points. If both players can say the verse from memory, they each receive another 100 points.
3. When all verses have been matched, collect the slips of paper and play the game again, as many times as you wish. The person with the highest overall score wins.

Motion Spelling

This game helps children learn to spell the names of characters, books, and important words from the Bible.

MEMORY VERSE
"Seek the Lord, and His strength."
— Psalm 105:4

PREPARATION
Choose a category or categories of words for the children to spell (books of the Bible, characters, places, etc.). For Bible books, use the list in the front of your Bible. Duplicate the list of Bible characters from the Word Search game on page 23, or make up a list of important Bible words such as salvation, faith, believe, etc. Place chairs in a row, side by side, one for each child.

HOW TO PLAY
1. Have the players stand side by side, in front of the chairs, facing you. After you read the first word, the first player in the line spells it. However, instead of saying the vowels, he must do the following motions:
   - A—raise right hand
   - E—raise left hand
   - I—point to eye
   - O—point to mouth while silently saying "oh"
   - U—point to leader

2. Each player spells one word during his turn, as in a spelling bee. If he spells the word correctly, he remains standing, and the next player in line spells the next word. If he misspells the word, he sits down. The last player standing is the winner.

3. After playing a few times, divide the children into two teams, one on each side of the room. If a player misses a word, the other team has an opportunity to spell it correctly. If they cannot spell it, their player must be seated. The game ends when one team's players are all seated. The other team wins.

Paper Plate Toss

This game helps children recall Bible stories that mention things which were thrown.

MEMORY VERSE

"Cast all your anxiety on Him because He cares for you." — I Peter 5:7 (NIV)

PREPARATION

You will need one heavyweight paper plate for each child and a copy of the Things in the Bible Which Were Thrown quiz from page 62. Mark a goal line about two feet from one end of the room with masking tape or chalk. At the other end of the room, at least ten feet away, if possible, mark another line (the base line).

HOW TO PLAY

1. Divide the players into two teams, and have them line up near the base line. One player from each team stands on the base line and attempts to throw a paper plate so that it lands on the goal line. The player whose plate comes closest to either side of the goal line must answer a question from the quiz.
2. If the player answers incorrectly, the other team's plate thrower may answer. Continue playing until each player has had a turn. If more questions are needed before the game ends, repeat some questions already given.
3. Award 100 points for the best throw and 200 points for a correct answer. The team with the highest score wins.
4. Discuss: What things in our lives do we sometimes feel like throwing away? Discuss the meaning of anxiety. What anxieties do you have? What does our memory verse say we should do with these cares and troubles? What do we need to do to cast them on God?
5. Give each child a paper plate. Have them write one of their anxieties on it. If possible, take the children outside, and let them throw their own plates as far as possible. (Have them pick up the plates following the prayer.) Ask them to pretend that they are throwing away their troubles. Close in prayer, thanking God for being with us and caring for us even when we have anxieties.

Avoiding Sins March

This game helps children talk about the right thing to do in situations where they are tempted to sin.

MEMORY VERSE

"Flee also youthful lusts: but follow righteousness, faith, charity, peace."
— II Timothy 2:22

PREPARATION
1. Fold newspaper pages in half. With a felt marker, print the name of a sin which the children might be tempted to do (lie, steal, cheat, curse, disobey parents, disobey teachers, be unkind to others, etc.) on each newspaper.
2. Place the folded newspapers on a carpeted floor or grass in a large circle, with an 8-inch space between each one. The circle must be big enough to allow each player to stand in an empty space between the newspapers. Bring a tape player and a music cassette or invite someone to play the piano or guitar (or have the leader clap).

HOW TO PLAY
1. Each player stands in a space between the papers. Tell the children that stepping on a paper means they have committed that sin. As music is played or the leader claps, everyone marches, trying to step in the spaces only.
2. When the music or clapping stops, anyone with

any part of his foot on a newspaper must name the sin and tell what a person should do instead of committing that sin. Then he must leave the circle and help watch for others who step on the newspaper. The last child remaining in the circle is the winner.

TO TALK ABOUT
Our memory verse says we should hurry away from youthful lusts. What are lusts? (desires for sinful things). Temptations are everywhere, but we should try to stay away from anything that could make it easier for us to sin (such as wearing your bathing suit to the lake when you're not supposed to go swimming). Can you name others?

Word Search

This game helps children learn to spell the names of Bible characters and to recall something significant about each character.

MEMORY VERSE

"Lord, Thou hast been our dwelling place in all generations." — Psalm 90:1

PREPARATION

Print the letters of Bible characters' names on 3 x 5-inch cards, one letter per card. Use the names below, or choose additional names with either four, five, or six letters. Print a number on each card to correspond with the character's name (Adam — A-1, D-1, A-1, M-1; Abel — A-2, B-2, E-2, L-2; etc.). Hide the cards around the room.

FOUR LETTERS: Adam, Abel, Cain, Esau, Noah, Amos, Mary, Paul, Luke, Mark, John, Boaz, Ruth, Joel, Saul.

FIVE LETTERS: Aaron, Abram, Sarah, Jacob, Isaac, Moses, Caleb, David, Jonah, Herod, James, Judas, Peter, Jesus, Satan.

SIX LETTERS: Joseph, Daniel, Samuel, Samson, Elijah, Elisha, Gideon, Esther, Isaiah, Joshua, Andrew, Martha, Thomas, Philip.

HOW TO PLAY

1. Give each player a number. At your signal, the players begin searching for cards with their number only. (If they find other cards, they must replace them.) Tell the players whether they are looking for names with four, five, or six letters.

2. When a player has found all his letters, he must then unscramble them to discover the name of his character. The first one to name his character and correctly spell the name is the winner. When all players have found their names, have each person tell one identifying fact about his character.

 # BIBLE KNOWLEDGE

Shouting Verses

This game will help children recall memory verses.

MEMORY VERSE

"Let all those that put their trust in Thee rejoice; let them ever shout for joy." — Psalm 5:11

PREPARATION

Bring a list of memory verses familiar to the children. If chairs are used, arrange them in two circles, one chair for each player.

HOW TO PLAY

1. Divide the players into two teams. Have each team sit in a circle in chairs or on the floor. Whisper one word of a memory verse to each player on the first team. If there are more players than words, give the same word to more than one player. If there are too many words, use as many words as you can. (Use enough words for the other team to understand the verse.)
2. At your signal, all members of the first team shout their words in unison. The second team has three chances to hear the shouts and guess the verse. If they guess correctly on the first shout, they earn 300 points. On the second shout, they get 200 points and on the third, 100 points.
3. The second team is given the next verse to shout. When all the verses have been used, the team with the highest score wins. You may want to repeat any verses that were not guessed correctly.

Bible Alphabet Cards

This game helps students learn to spell frequently used Bible words and names of Bible characters.

MEMORY VERSE

"Thy law do I love." — Psalm 119:113

PREPARATION

With a black marker, print each letter of the alphabet on a 3 x 5-inch card, one letter per card. Print two cards for each vowel and two cards for the letter "s". Print letters as large as you can make them. Prepare two identical sets of 3 x 5-inch cards, one for each team. Provide a table for each team.

HOW TO PLAY

1. Lay a set of letters, face up, on each table, leaving room near the edge for spelling the word. Divide the players into two teams. Have them sit or stand near their letters. Choose a captain for each team, to position the letters to spell the words.
2. Call out a word from the list below (or make up your own words):

Adam	Mark
Eve	Luke
Noah	John
Mary	Isaac
Paul	heaven
Jacob	Spirit
Joseph	create
Moses	holy
Joshua	heart
Samuel	soul
Daniel	saved
Jesus	salvation
Christ	repent
Lord	

   The players on each team confer on the spelling and find the correct letters. The captain arranges the letters and then calls out, "Done!" The other team continues to spell, in case the first team has a misspelled the word.
3. The first team with the correct spelling gets 100 points. Continue until all the words have been spelled. The team with the most points wins.

Buzz-Bing

This game helps children recall well-known Bible characters.

MEMORY VERSE

"I press toward the mark for the prize of the high calling of God in Christ Jesus."
— Philippians 3:14

PREPARATION

If chairs are used, provide one for each player. You will need a copy of the Who Was I? quiz from page 62.

HOW TO PLAY

1. Divide the players into two teams. Have players sit with their team members, in chairs or on the floor. Give one team the sound "Buzz" to call out, and give the other "Bing." Ask a quiz question. Any player who thinks he knows the answer calls out the sound for his team. *Only* that player may give the answer.
2. If the player answers correctly, his team earns 100 points. If he answers incorrectly, his team loses 100 points. If a team has no points, no additional points can be deducted, until the team once again has points. If a player can give the Bible reference as well as the answer, his team earns an additional 100 points.
3. If "Buzz" and "Bing" are called out simultaneously, both players may whisper their an-swers to a leader. Each team earns 100 points if they are correct. A team that answers incorrectly loses 100 points.
4. Continue until all questions have been asked. Feel free to repeat questions which were not answered correctly. The team with the most points at the end of the game wins.

ANOTHER WAY TO PLAY

Use this game to review memory verses and their Scripture references. Play as above, but state the Scripture reference for a memory verse. Any player who thinks he knows the answer calls out the sound for his team. *Only* that player may give the answer.

Jail Break!

This game reviews the story of Peter's miraculous escape from prison (Acts 12).

MEMORY VERSE

"Peter therefore was kept in prison: but prayer was made without ceasing of the church unto God for him." — Acts 12:5

PREPARATION

Make two copies of the game board and Peter playing piece from page 28 (one copy for each team). Cut out the playing pieces. Glue each game board inside a file folder on the right hand side. On the left, glue a small envelope to hold the playing piece. For individuals to compete against each other, make a board and a playing piece for each player. You will need two tables or floor space for this game.

HOW TO PLAY

1. Before playing the game the first time, tell the story of Peter's escape from prison (Acts 12) in detail. Emphasize the answers to the quiz questions.
2. Divide the players into two teams. Give each team a game board and Peter playing piece. Each team decides which player will begin. Choose a team to start. Alternate asking the teams Jail Break Questions from below, moving from player to player within each team in a clockwise direction.
3. If a player answers the question correctly, the team may move Peter forward one square. If the player answers incorrectly, the team must put Peter back one square, and the other team has a chance to answer that question. The first team to help Peter break out of jail wins. If the questions run out before Peter breaks out of jail, repeat them.

ANOTHER WAY TO PLAY

1. Divide the players into smaller teams of two or three players. Give each team a game board and playing piece. Play as above, but let team members collaborate on their answers.
2. If a team gives an incorrect answer, the other teams are not given a chance to answer it. However, those questions may be repeated later in the game. The first team to help Peter break out of jail wins.

JAIL BREAK QUESTIONS

1. Who was put in prison? (Peter)
2. Why was Peter put in prison? (For preaching God's Word)
3. Which king put Peter in prison? (Herod)
4. How many chains held Peter? (Two)
5. What were Peter's friends doing that night? (Praying)
6. Who came to rescue Peter? (An angel)
7. What happened when Peter stood up? (Chains fell off)
8. What did Peter's rescuer tell Peter to put on his feet? (Sandals)
9. What opened by itself for Peter? (Iron gate)
10. Where did Peter go when he escaped? (His friend's house — to Mary, John's mother)
11. Who came to the door when Peter knocked? (Rhoda)
12. When the servant girl saw Peter, what did she do? (Left him standing there while she ran back into the house)
13. Whom did Peter's friends think the servant girl had seen? (His angel)
14. What did the king do to the soldiers that had guarded Peter? (Had them killed.)
15. When the king let people worship him and call him a god, what happened to him? (He was eaten by worms and died.)

Peter goes past one guard.

Peter goes past second guard.

Iron gate opens.

FREEDOM!

Peter goes out prison door.

Another soldier sleeps.

One soldier sleeps.

Peter puts on his cloak.

Peter puts on his sandals.

Another chain falls off.

One chain falls off.

"Get up, Peter!"

START

Playing Instructions:
Divide the players into two teams, and give each team a game board and Peter playing piece. Each team decides which player will begin. Choose a team to start. Alternate questions between the two teams, moving from player to player in a clockwise direction. If a player answers the question correctly, the team may move their Peter playing piece forward one square. If the player answers incorrectly, the team must move Peter back a square, and the other team has a chance to answer the question. The first team to help Peter break out of jail wins.

JAIL BREAK!

Let's Go Fishing

This game helps children recall Bible stories involving fish and encourages them to become fishers of men.

MEMORY VERSE

"Follow Me, and I will make you fishers of men." — Matthew 4:19

PREPARATION

You will need a copy of the Fishing Quiz from page 63 and sixteen 3 x 5-inch cards. Duplicate the fish and shark patterns from below. Glue a fish on most of the cards. On a few, glue a shark. (Count the number of shark cards.) Place all the cards in a paper bag. Provide each team with a bucket or a large container (a bowl, frying pan, etc.)

HOW TO PLAY

1. Divide the players into two teams: 1) Peter and Andrew and 2) James and John. A player from one team takes a card from the bag. If it is a fish, he must answer a question. If it is a shark, his team must give one of their fish (if they have one) to the other team.

2. If a player answers the question correctly, he places the fish in his team's bucket. If he answers incorrectly, he returns the fish to the bag. The other team then has a turn to fish. Continue until all fish (except sharks) have been caught. The team with the most fish wins.

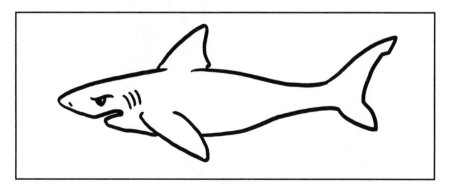

Twenty Pennies Quiz

This quiz game reminds children that God condemns the love of money.

MEMORY VERSE

"The love of money is the root of all evil." — I Timothy 6:10

PREPARATION

Duplicate the quiz, What the Bible Says About Money, from page 63. You will need 40 pennies.

HOW TO PLAY

1. Divide the players into two teams. Have the teams stand in two lines, facing each other. Place 20 pennies on the floor in front of each team. Ask the first player of one team a question from the quiz. If he answers correctly, the other team is asked a question. If he answers incorrectly, he must take a penny from his team and give it to the other team.

2. Continue asking a question of each team, until all questions have been asked. Repeat any questions that were not answered correctly the first time. The team with the most pennies at the end of the game wins.

Who Am I?

This game helps children learn and remember facts about people of the Bible.

MEMORY VERSE

"Choose you this day whom ye will serve ... but as for me and my house, we will serve the Lord." — Joshua 24:15

PREPARATION

If chairs are used, arrange them in a semi-circle, one for each player except It.

HOW TO PLAY

1. Choose one player to be It, and send him from the room. The remaining players sit in a semi-circle and choose a Bible character. Bring It back into the room. He must go to each person and ask, "Who am I?"

2. Each player whom he asks must answer with one fact about the Bible character. When It guesses correctly, the last person to give a clue is the next It. A player who is not able to give a clue becomes It. Continue playing until most players have been It.

Conquest

This game helps children recognize the main cities of Israel's conquests and learn some promises from the Book of Joshua.

MEMORY VERSE

"The Lord your God fights for you, just as He promised." — Joshua 23:10 (NIV)

PREPARATION

1. Make one Conquest game for every five or six players. Duplicate the game pattern from pages 32 and 33, and glue it inside a file folder. Laminate the folder or cover it with clear adhesive-backed plastic. Cut a 2 3/8 x 3 1/2-inch rectangle from construction paper and glue it to the game board, as marked, for a pocket to hold the game pieces.

2. Duplicate the Joshua tokens and the game cards from page 34. Cut the tokens apart. Color them different colors. Glue them to cardboard. Cut eighteen 3 x 5-inch index cards in half. Glue each game card to half an index card. Laminate the tokens and cards or cover them with clear, adhesive-backed plastic. Place the set of cards in a small paper grocery bag. Provide a table and chairs or a large open space on the floor for this game. Each team will need a Bible.

HOW TO PLAY

1. Place the game board on a table or the floor. Put the bag of cards nearby. Give each player a Joshua playing piece. Explain that players will follow Israel's conquests of Canaan from the time Israel crossed the Jordan River until the land had rest from war. All players begin with their Joshua playing pieces on START. Decide who will begin, and continue around the table clockwise.

2. Each player draws one game card from the bag and moves the number of spaces indicated. If there is a Scripture reference on the card, he must look it up and read it aloud before moving. After reading the card, the player places it in a discard pile on the table.

3. When a player lands on a space with words, he follows those directions. If all the cards have been drawn before the game is done, replace them in the bag. The first "Joshua" to reach FINISH wins the game.

ANOTHER WAY TO PLAY THIS GAME

1. Play the game with two teams. Each team has one Joshua playing piece. Players take turns drawing the cards and moving their team's Joshua, following the directions above.

2. When a team lands on a space with a city or event, that player must describe the actions that took place in the city during the event. The team gets another turn if they describe the event correctly. If they describe it incorrectly, their turn ends. The first team to reach FINISH wins the game.

Conquest

Playing Instructions:

Place the game board on a table or the floor. Put the game cards in a bag beside the game board. Give each player a Joshua playing piece. All players begin with their Joshua playing pieces on START. Decide who will begin, and continue around the table, clockwise. Each player draws one game card from the bag and moves the number of spaces indicated. If there is a verse on the card, he must read it aloud before moving. After reading the card, the player places it in a discard pile on the table. When a player lands in a space with words, he follows those directions. If all the cards are drawn before the game is done, replace them in the bag. The first "Joshua" to reach FINISH wins.

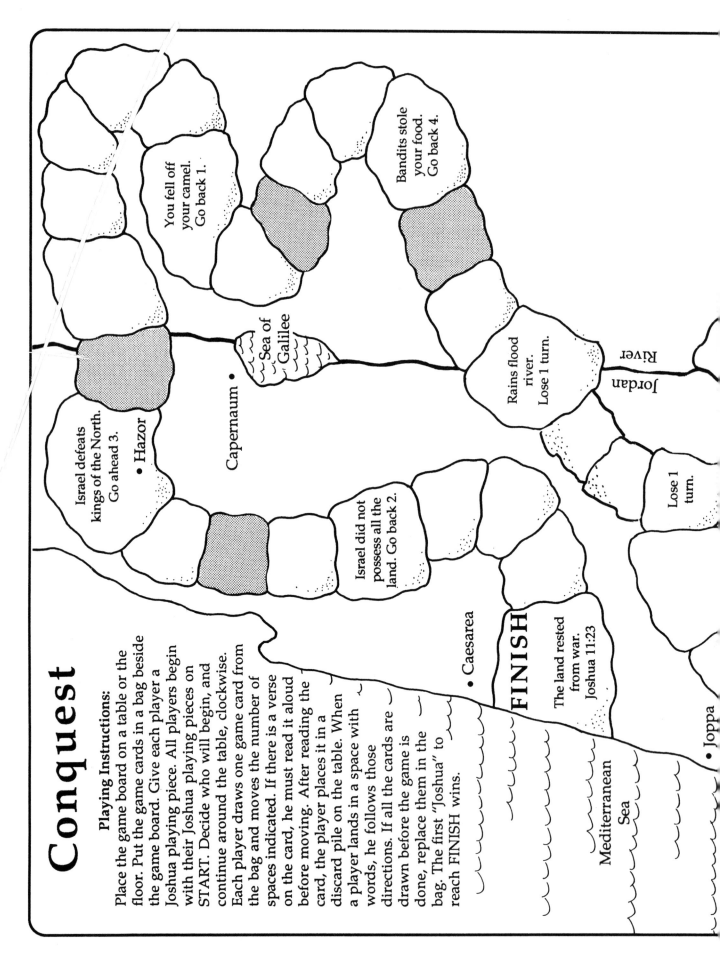

You fell off your camel. Go back 1.

Bandits stole your food. Go back 4.

Israel defeats kings of the North. Go ahead 3.

• Hazor

• Capernaum

Sea of Galilee

Rains flood river. Lose 1 turn.

Jordan River

Lose 1 turn.

Israel did not possess all the land. Go back 2.

• Caesarea

FINISH

The land rested from war. Joshua 11:23

Mediterranean Sea

• Joppa

32

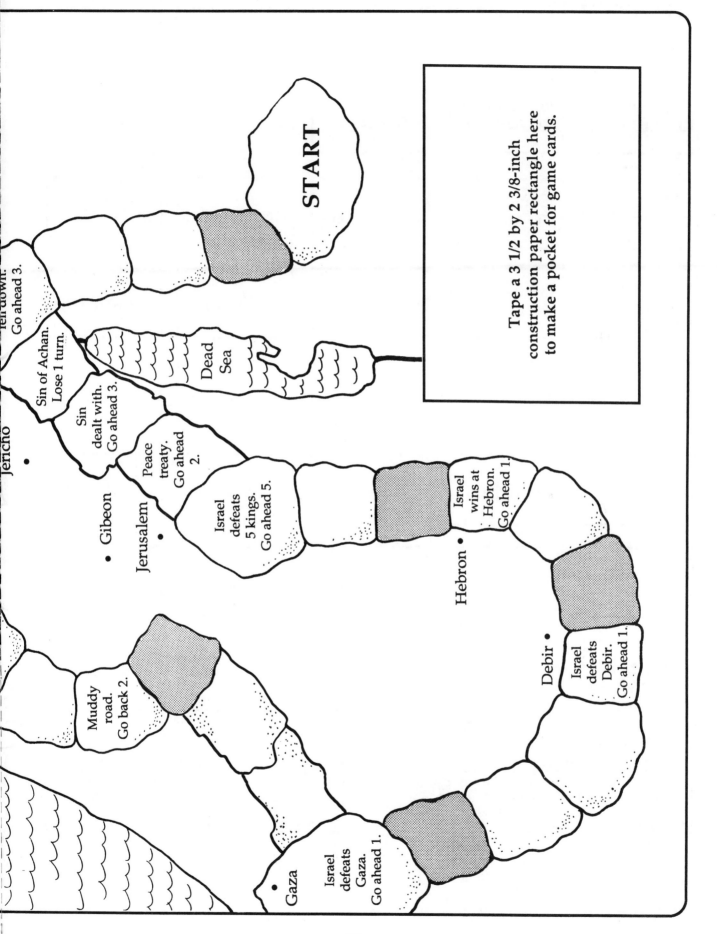

START

Tape a 3 1/2 by 2 3/8-inch construction paper rectangle here to make a pocket for game cards.

Dead Sea

fell down.
Go ahead 3.

Sin of Achan.
Lose 1 turn.

Sin dealt with.
Go ahead 3.

Jericho

Peace treaty.
Go ahead 2.

Gibeon

Jerusalem

Israel defeats 5 kings. Go ahead 5.

Israel wins at Hebron.
Go ahead 1.

Hebron

Debir

Israel defeats Debir.
Go ahead 1.

Muddy road.
Go back 2.

Gaza

Israel defeats Gaza.
Go ahead 1.

Joshua 1:2 GO AHEAD 4	Joshua 23:8 GO AHEAD 4	GO AHEAD 1	GO AHEAD 2	GO AHEAD 3
Joshua 1:3 GO AHEAD 4	Joshua 23:11 GO AHEAD 4	GO AHEAD 1	GO AHEAD 2	GO AHEAD 3
Joshua 1:5 GO AHEAD 4	Joshua 23:10 GO AHEAD 4	GO AHEAD 1	GO AHEAD 2	GO AHEAD 3
Joshua 1:9 GO AHEAD 4	Joshua 24:15 GO AHEAD 4	GO AHEAD 1	GO AHEAD 2	GO AHEAD 3
Joshua 1:16 GO AHEAD 4	GO AHEAD 1	GO AHEAD 1	GO AHEAD 2	GO AHEAD 3
Joshua 1:13 GO AHEAD 4	GO AHEAD 1	GO AHEAD 1	GO AHEAD 2	GO AHEAD 3
Joshua 4:22 GO AHEAD 4	GO AHEAD 1	GO AHEAD 2	GO AHEAD 2	GO AHEAD 3
Joshua 23:3 GO AHEAD 4	GO AHEAD 1	GO AHEAD 2	GO AHEAD 2	GO AHEAD 3

SING-A-LONG GAMES

Penny Pass

This song and game teach children that God asks them to be good friends. It is also a fun get-acquainted activity.

MEMORY VERSE

"Greet the friends by name." — III John 14

PREPARATION

For this game you will need a penny and a small gift for each child (a balloon, a cookie, etc.). Bring a tape player and music cassette or invite someone to play the piano or guitar. Before the game begins, secretly give one player the penny.

HOW TO PLAY

1. Have the players stand where they may move about freely. As music is played, the players shake hands with each other. The person with the penny counts five handshakes and gives the penny to the fifth person. That person, in turn, gives it to the fifth person who shakes his hand, and so on.
2. When the music stops, the child with the penny holds it up for all to see. Everyone sings DO YOU KNOW THE BIBLE VERSE to the tune of DO YOU KNOW THE MUFFIN MAN?

3. The child holding the penny must say the memory verse. If he does so correctly, he returns the penny to the teacher and receives a prize.
4. If he says the verse incorrectly, he returns the penny to the teacher but does not receive a prize. The teacher then pretends to drop the penny in someone's hand. After actually dropping the penny, the teacher should continue to pretend with a few more children. When the music begins, the game resumes. (Once the memory verse has been said several times, choose a new verse, and continue playing.)

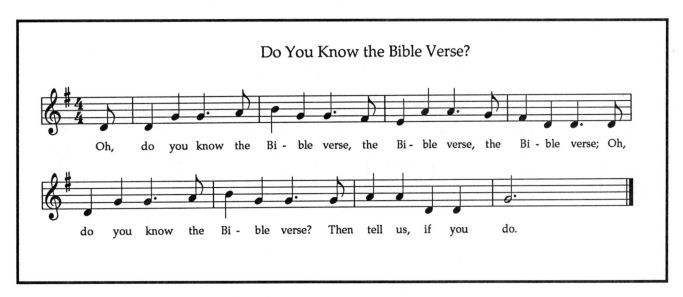

Do You Know the Bible Verse?

Oh, do you know the Bi - ble verse, the Bi - ble verse, the Bi - ble verse; Oh,

do you know the Bi - ble verse? Then tell us, if you do.

Drop Out

This game and song help children understand that trusting Jesus as their Savior is the only way to go to heaven.

MEMORY VERSE

"For God so loved the world, that He gave His only begotten Son, that whosoever believeth in Him should not perish, but have everlasting life." — John 3:16

PREPARATION

Draw a large circle in the playing area with chalk or masking tape. Or, in a small room, the circle may be around the perimeter of the room. Tape two or more open newspapers around the circle, more for a large circle with many participants. Teach the song, and then play the game as directed.

HOW TO PLAY

1. The leader and the children line up around the circle and sing CHILDREN, CHILDREN, I'VE BEEN THINKING. (The music is below.) The leader sings the first verse, the children sing the second, and everyone sings the third.

CHILDREN, CHILDREN, I'VE BEEN THINKING

1) Children, children, I've been thinking,
    Oh, how happy I would be,
   If some day you'd go to heaven,
    Where you'd live eternally.

2) Teacher, Teacher, we've been thinking,
    Oh, how happy we would be,
   If some day we'd go to heaven,
    Where we'd live eternally.

3) Jesus died so we could go there,
    And He is the only Way;
   If we trust Him as our Savior,
    He will take us there some day.

2. Pause at the end of each verse. On the last word, those left standing with any part of a foot on a newspaper must drop out of the game (including the leader). No slowing down or stopping allowed before the song ends! Stop the game when you wish or let it continue until one player is left. Those still in the circle at the end are the winners.

Children, Children, I've Been Thinking

Chil - dren, chil - dren, I've been think- ing, Oh, how hap - py I would be,

If some day you'd go to heav - en, Where you'd live e - ter - nal - ly.

Go and Tell

This game and song teach children that Christians are responsible for telling others the gospel message.

MEMORY VERSE

"Go ye into all the world, and preach the gospel to every creature." — Mark 16:15

PREPARATION

Print the names of some countries from around the world on small slips of red construction paper, one name per paper. Repeat the same names on yellow construction paper slips, one name per slip. Make as many total slips (red and yellow) as you have players. (Make several extras for visitors.) You will need masking tape and two Bibles or New Testaments.

HOW TO PLAY

1. Teach children the memory verse and the song, GO AND TELL. Divide the players into two teams, the Reds and the Golds. Tape a red slip on the chest of each Red Team member and a yellow slip on each Gold member. Have the two teams mill around, mixing together. Then they should spread out, leaving as much space as possible between players.
2. Give a Bible to one member of each team and say, "Go." They must find another member of their own team, give him the Bible, and sit down. Each player who received the Bible takes

it to another member of his team (one who is standing), and sits down.
3. The object is to see which team "carries the gospel" faster. Continue until all members of one team are seated. The first team with all of its members seated is the winner.
4. While they are seated, let the children think of ways they could help get the gospel to people in other countries. Discuss ways they could share the gospel in their own neighborhoods.
5. Sing GO AND TELL to the tune of ROW, ROW, ROW YOUR BOAT. (The music is below.) When the children know the song well, sing it in a round. Divide the children into small groups, each of which will sing the song in turn. All groups should sing through the song at least three times.

Go and Tell

Go, go, go and tell; We've good news to share;

Je - sus died up - on the cross for peo - ple ev - 'ry - where.

Come On, Children

This game and song stress the importance of going to church, even when children may be tempted to do otherwise.

MEMORY VERSE

"Come ye, and let us go up to . . . the house of . . . God." — Isaiah 2:3

PREPARATION

With chalk, tape, or a line drawn in the sand, mark two goal lines, one at each end of the playing area.

HOW TO PLAY

1. Have the children stand behind one of the goal lines. Explain that this line represents home and the other represents church. Choose one child to be It. He represents a bad influence and stands between the two lines.

2. The players wait behind the home line and sing the first lines of COME ON, CHILDREN to the tune of GOODNIGHT, LADIES. (The music is below.) On the word "joyfully," they begin to walk slowly toward the church line, singing the remainder of the song. When they finish the song, they break into a run, with It tagging as many as he can.

3. Those who are caught by It must try to help It catch the others as the game starts again. (Reverse the home and church lines with each play.) Continue until only one player remains free or until all are caught.

Come On, Children

Come on, chil-dren; come on, chil-dren;

Come on, chil-dren; It's time for church, you know.

Joy-ful-ly we walk a-long, walk a-long, walk a-long;

Joy-ful-ly we walk a-long, as off to church we go.

What's Missing?

This game teaches children the names of the disciples. It can also be used to teach the tribes of Israel or the books of the Bible.

MEMORY VERSE

"If ye continue in My Word, then are ye My disciples indeed."
— John 8:31

PREPARATION

Print the names of the disciples on 3 x 5-inch cards, one name per card. You will need a table and an area away from the table for the players to sit or stand.

HOW TO PLAY

1. Teach the song, THE BIBLE IS THE WORD OF GOD, and review the names of the disciples before playing the game. Place the cards on the table, face up. Divide the players into two teams. They may stand or sit with their backs to the table. Remove one disciple card from the table, while everyone sings these words to the tune of LONDON BRIDGE: (The music is below.)

   THE BIBLE IS THE WORD OF GOD
   The Bible is the Word of God,
     Word of God, Word of God;
   The Bible is the Word of God.
     Do you know it?

2. When the song ends, the first two players, one from each team, go to the table, look at the cards, and name the disciple card that is missing. The first player to do this correctly wins 100 points for his team. (You may want to limit their chances to respond to two or three.)

3. If they are not able to name the missing disciple card, two new players come to the table and try to name it. The first player to name it correctly wins 100 points for his team. Replace the missing card and remove another one for the next two players (or pretend to remove another card, but remove the same one).

4. Continue until all children have had a turn. The team with the most points wins. When children have mastered the game, remove two or more cards at once.

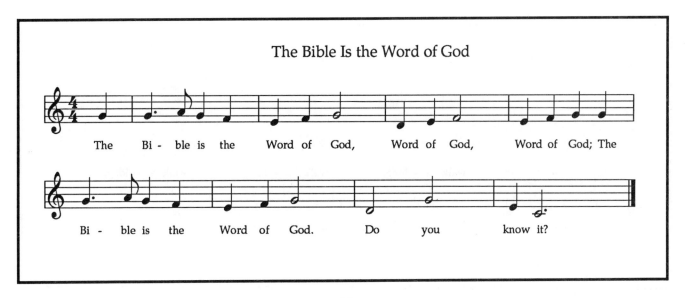

The Bible Is the Word of God

The Bi - ble is the Word of God, Word of God, Word of God; The

Bi - ble is the Word of God. Do you know it?

Gospel Colors

This song and game teach children the plan of salvation.

MEMORY VERSE

"The gospel . . . is the power of God for the salvation of everyone who believes." — Romans 1:16 (NIV)

PREPARATION

Cut pieces of red, gold, black, and white construction paper in half. You will need one rectangle paper of each color. Teach the song GOSPEL COLORS, and discuss the meaning of the gospel colors. Have children memorize the scripture verse to be used with each color. (The music and verses are below.) When most of the children know the meanings and verses, play the game.

HOW TO PLAY

1. Players may sit or stand in a circle. Give the colored papers to four different children, spaced around the circle.
2. Sing the song, GOSPEL COLORS. As the song is sung, the colors are passed from one player to another. When the song ends, those holding a color must tell its meaning and give the verse. If they are incorrect, they drop out of the game, but continue to sing the song.
3. Continue playing until there are only four players left. Those who can give the meaning of the color they hold and its verse are the winners.

GOSPEL COLOR MEANINGS & VERSES:

1) BLACK — Sin (Romans 1:21 and Ephesians 5:8). Verse: *"For all have sinned, and come short of the glory of God."* — Romans 3:23
2) RED — The blood of Christ (I Peter 2:24 and I John 1:7). Verse: *"While we were yet sinners, Christ died for us."* — Romans 5:8
3) WHITE — The clean heart after Jesus comes into it (Psalm 51:7). Verse: *"Believe in the Lord Jesus, and you will be saved."* — Acts 16:31 (NIV)
4) GOLD — Heaven (John 14:1-6). Verse: *"Whosoever shall call upon the name of the Lord shall be saved."* — Romans 10:13.

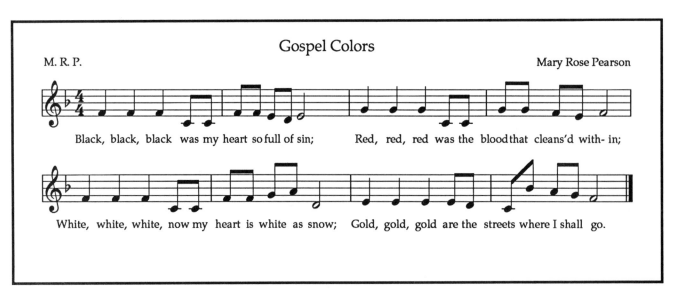

Each One Bring One

This game and song teach children that Christians, even Christian children, can bring others to the Lord.

MEMORY VERSE

"He that winneth souls is wise."
— Proverbs 11:30

PREPARATION

Mark a goal line at one end of the room or playing area and a starting line at the other end. Leave room for the players to stand in single file behind the starting line.

HOW TO PLAY

1. Teach the children the song, THE CHRISTIAN TELLS A FRIEND. Divide the players into two or more teams with no more than twelve members to a team. Choose one player from each team to be the Christian and stand behind the goal line. The other players (sinners) form lines by team, behind the starting line. Tell the children that the goal line represents salvation.
2. All team members (sinners) sing these words to the tune of THE FARMER IN THE DELL: (The music is below.)

THE CHRISTIAN TELLS A FRIEND
The Christian tells a friend,
   The Christian tells a friend,
"Jesus died for all your sins,"
   The Christian tells a friend.

As they sing, each Christian runs to his team, takes the hand of the first sinner, and brings him or her to the goal line. This second person runs back to the starting line and brings the next person to the goal. (The runners' hands must stay clasped.)
3. Once they have brought a friend to the goal, the new Christians sing along with the remaining sinners. Continue until every sinner on the team has reached salvation. The first team with all of its players across the goal line wins.
4. At this point, all Christians cross to the remaining sinners, everyone joins hands and walks to the goal line singing the final verse:
   They all tell some more,
      They all tell some more,
   "Jesus died for all your sins,"
      They all tell some more.

The Christian Tells a Friend

The Chris-tian tells a friend, ___ The Chris-tian tells a friend,
"Je - sus died for all your sins," the Chris-tian tells a friend.

Going Up

This game and song teach children that Jesus is the only way to heaven.

MEMORY VERSE

"I am the Way, the Truth, and the Life: no man cometh unto the Father, but by Me."
— John 14:6

PREPARATION

Mark a starting line and a goal line with chalk, tape, or in some other way, at least ten or twelve feet apart.

HOW TO PLAY

1. All players stand at the starting line. The leader stands at the goal line, which represents heaven. The object is to see who can reach the goal line first.
2. The leader calls out ways by which people hope to get to heaven. The players may take a step only when the leader says, "Jesus is the Way." When other ways are named, they may lift a foot; but anyone who steps ahead must go back to the starting line. The ways should be named quickly enough to keep the game interesting.
3. Some ways to call out might be: church is the Way, being good is the Way, baptism is the Way, obeying the commandments is the Way, helping others is the Way.
4. Continue until all players reach the goal line. Then sing, GOING UP: (The music is below.)

GOING UP
Do you want to go up, up, up,
   Up to heaven above?
Then trust the One who came down, down, down,
   Down to save you in love.

5. To use motions with the song, raise hands and body upward on the word "up," going higher each time. Come back down gradually on the word "down."

Going Up

M. R. P.

Mary Rose Pearson

Do you want to go up, up, up, Up to heav- en a - bove? Then trust the One who came down, down, down, Down to save you in love.

PAPER & PENCIL GAMES

Bible Kings Squares

This game helps children become familiar with the names of Bible kings.

MEMORY VERSE

"Behold, a king shall reign in righteousness." — Isaiah 32:1

PREPARATION

Photocopy one game sheet from page 44 for every two players. Bring a pencil for each player. Provide a hard writing surface for the game.

HOW TO PLAY

1. Before playing, review the names of each king on the first two rows of the game sheet. (The names are repeated on subsequent rows.) Let the children take turns pronouncing the names and telling something about each king.
2. Divide the children into pairs. (If you have an uneven number of children, pair an adult with one child, or form some teams of three.) Give each player a pencil, and give each team a game sheet. Players take turns drawing one vertical or horizontal line to connect two dots. (Players may connect no more than two dots per turn.)
3. If the line drawn completes a square, that player scores the number of points shown in the Key. Each time a player completes a square, he writes his initials in it and takes another turn. The object is to complete as many boxes as possible, while preventing the other player from completing boxes.
4. The player with the most points after all boxes are drawn wins. If desired, the teams may compete against each other to see which team can complete the puzzle first.

KEY

Jesus	=	1000 points
David	=	500 points
Solomon	=	400 points
Hezekiah	=	300 points
All others	=	100 points

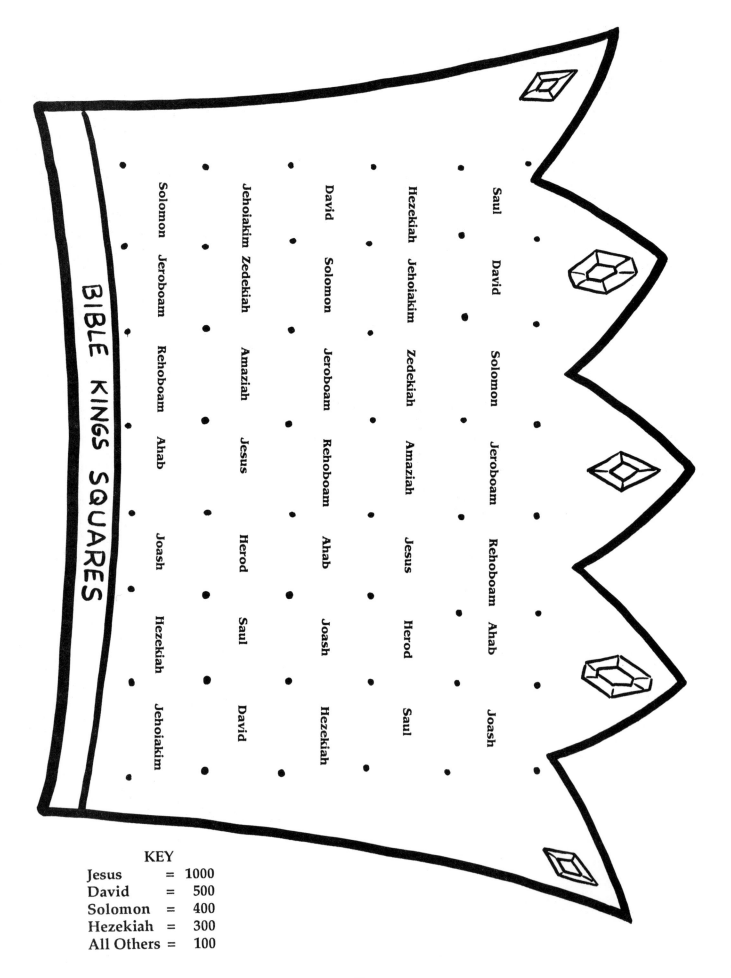

BIBLE KINGS SQUARES

							Saul
						Hezekiah	David
					David	Jehoiakim	Solomon
			Solomon	Jehoiakim	Solomon	Zedekiah	Jeroboam
		Solomon	Jeroboam	Zedekiah	Jeroboam	Amaziah	Rehoboam
		Jeroboam	Rehoboam	Amaziah	Rehoboam	Jesus	Ahab
		Rehoboam	Ahab	Jesus	Ahab	Herod	Joash
		Ahab	Joash	Herod	Joash	Saul	
		Joash	Hezekiah	Saul	Hezekiah	David	
		Hezekiah	Jehoiakim	David			

KEY

Jesus	=	1000
David	=	500
Solomon	=	400
Hezekiah	=	300
All Others	=	100

44

Bible Baseball

This quiz game helps children remember the places where major Bible events took place.

MEMORY VERSE

"All Scripture is given by inspiration of God." — II Timothy 3:16

PREPARATION

Duplicate the Where Did It Happen? Quiz from page 64. Duplicate the game board pattern from page 46 two times. (You will need one game board for each team. Very large groups may want to have three or more teams.) Laminate the game boards or cover them with clear, adhesive-backed plastic. Bring eight checkers, buttons, or small squares of cardboard for playing pieces and two grease pencils for score keeping (four playing pieces and one grease pencil per team). Provide two tables, or use the floor.

HOW TO PLAY

1. Divide the children into two teams (or more, for large groups), and seat the team members together (at a table or on the floor). Give each team a grease pencil, four playing pieces (baseball players) and a game board (playing field). Before beginning, decide how many innings will be played and which team will be up to bat first.
2. Each team writes the inning number at the bottom of their game board. The team up to bat chooses a player (the batter) to answer the first question. If he answers correctly, he places a baseball player (playing piece) on first base.
3. If he answers incorrectly, he is out, and his turn ends. The next player on that team becomes the batter and attempts to answer a question. Continue until three outs are scored. After three outs, the other team is up to bat.
4. A baseball player on any base is moved forward when a question is answered correctly. A run is scored when a baseball player reaches home base. Each team records their runs at the bottom of their game board. Continue playing until the specified number of innings have been completed. The team with the most runs at the end of all innings wins.

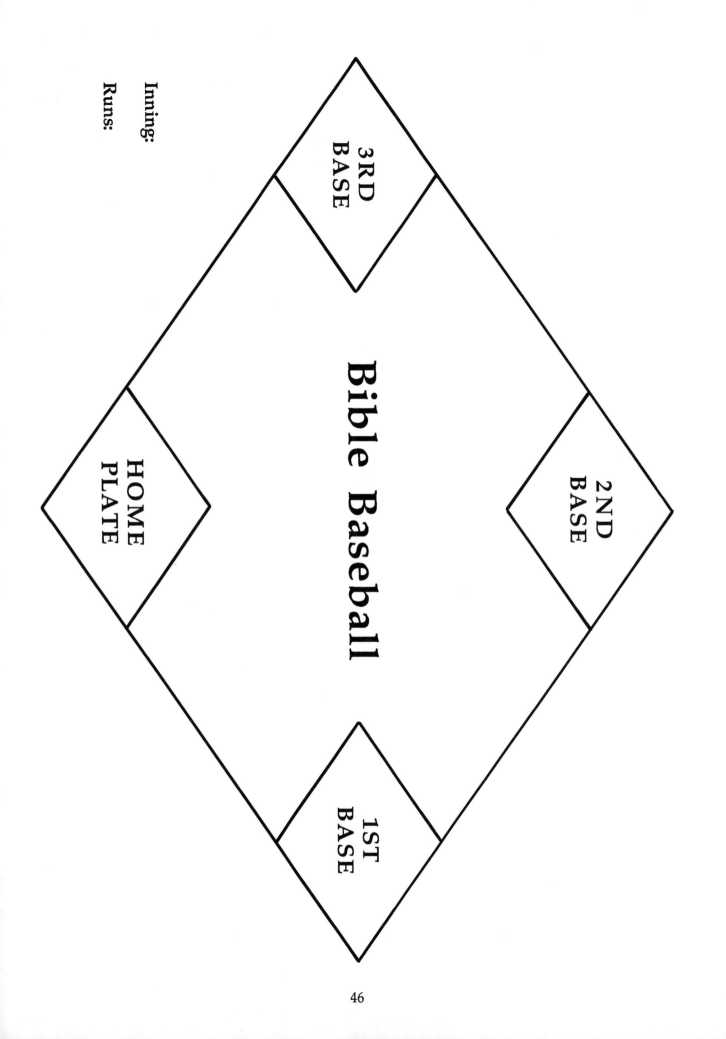

Bible Baseball

3RD BASE

2ND BASE

HOME PLATE

1ST BASE

Inning:

Runs:

46

A Message from Bible Characters

This game helps children recognize the names of well-known people from the Bible.

MEMORY VERSE

"Blessed are they that hear the Word of God, and keep it." — Luke 11:28

PREPARATION

Duplicate the game sheet from page 48, one for every two or three children. Each child will need a pencil and each team will need a Bible. Provide a table or a hard writing surface for this game.

HOW TO PLAY

1. Review the names of the Bible characters listed on the game sheet. Say the name aloud, and discuss that character's accomplishments and failures with the children.
2. Divide the children into teams of two or three, and give each team a game sheet and a Bible. Give each child a pencil. Explain that the words in the squares on the game sheet are all names of people. Players on each team should take turns circling those which are the names of Bible characters.
3. When they are finished, players may take turns printing the first letter of the remaining names in the blanks below (from left to right). If the game has been completed correctly, they will have a message from the Bible characters. (This is something the Bible characters might say if they met you.) The first team to correctly complete the puzzle (without using their Bible) wins. After playing, have teams use their Bibles to check their answers.

PUZZLE ANSWERS

Names that should not be circled:

Bob	Lily	Stacy
Evelyn	Larry	Opie
Yancy	Owen	Freda
Earnest	Woody	Gary
Fred	Elise	Otis
Opal	Roger	Dick

Bible Characters Message:
Be ye followers of God. (from Ephesians 5:1)

A Message from Bible Characters

Circle the names of the Bible characters in the squares below.

PETER	EVE	BOB	ZACCHAEUS	EVELYN	PAUL	YANCY
EARNEST	AARON	NOAH	MARY	MARK	FRED	OPAL
HANNAH	ELIJAH	LILY	ISAAC	JOSEPH	LARRY	ABEL
OWEN	LOT	JAMES	AMOS	ESTHER	WOODY	JOSHUA
ELISE	DANIEL	JOHN	GIDEON	ROGER	STACY	LAZARUS
OPIE	ISAIAH	ABRAHAM	DAVID	FREDA	GARY	ADAM
MARTHA	OTIS	AMOS	SAMUEL	DICK	SARAH	THOMAS

Print the first letter of the uncircled names from left to right in the blanks below to reveal a message from the Bible characters.

___ __ __ __ __ __ __ __ __ __ __ __ __ __ __ __ __ __ __

(from Ephesians 5:1)

The Good Example Goal

This game helps children think about whether their actions are good or bad examples to others.

MEMORY VERSE

"Be thou an example of the believers."
— I Timothy 4:12

PREPARATION

Duplicate enough game sheets from page 50 so that every 2 to 6 players may have one. Color the game, if you wish, and back it with cardboard. Laminate it or cover it with clear adhesive-backed plastic. Duplicate the square patterns below five times for each game, color and laminate them, if desired, and mount them on cardboard. Place the squares in a cloth bag or a small paper grocery bag. Each player will need a penny, a bean, or some other small object for a marker.

HOW TO PLAY

1. Explain that all Christians should try to be good examples to others. When people see a good example, they are encouraged to trust Christ and to become more like Him. Discuss ways that children can be good examples (sharing a treat, being kind, helping out parents, greeting someone who is new at school, etc.).

2. Divide the children into teams of 2 to 6 players. Give each team a game sheet, and give each player a marker. Each player, in turn, draws a number from the bag, replaces it, and moves that many spaces on the game sheet.

3. If a player lands on a space with words, he must read the words aloud, and decide whether that activity would be a good or bad example. He must then move ahead or back according to its directions. The team that reaches the Good Example Goal first wins.

49

The Good Example Game

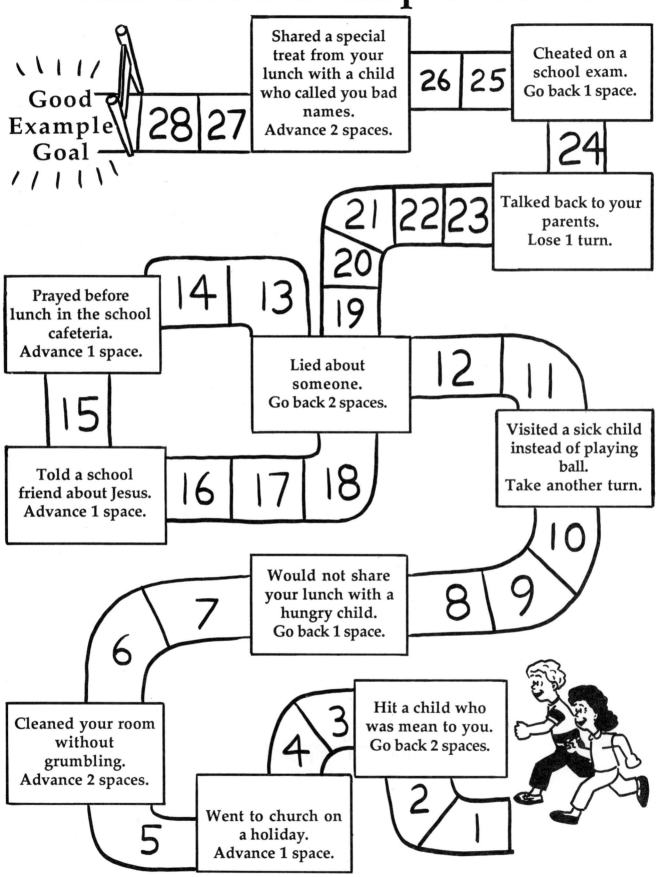

Good Example Goal

28 27

Shared a special treat from your lunch with a child who called you bad names. Advance 2 spaces.

26 25

Cheated on a school exam. Go back 1 space.

24

21 22 23

Talked back to your parents. Lose 1 turn.

20 19

14 13

Prayed before lunch in the school cafeteria. Advance 1 space.

Lied about someone. Go back 2 spaces.

12 11

15

Visited a sick child instead of playing ball. Take another turn.

Told a school friend about Jesus. Advance 1 space.

16 17 18

10

Would not share your lunch with a hungry child. Go back 1 space.

8 9

7

6

Cleaned your room without grumbling. Advance 2 spaces.

4 3

Hit a child who was mean to you. Go back 2 spaces.

2

1

5

Went to church on a holiday. Advance 1 space.

God's Plan of Salvation

This puzzle helps children understand the plan of salvation.

MEMORY VERSE

"Christ Jesus came into the world to save sinners."
— I Timothy 1:15

PREPARATION

You will need a copy of the puzzle from page 52, a pencil, and a Bible for each child. Provide a table or a hard surface for writing.

HOW TO PLAY

1. Give each child a Bible, a pencil, and a puzzle page. Begin with a sword drill: call out each Scripture reference on the puzzle page, and see who can find it first. Have that child read the verse aloud.
2. Direct children to read the first sentence on their puzzle page. Help them decide which word from the Scripture verse will fit in the blank. Read the verse again, if necessary. As they discover the missing word, they may write it in the blank. Continue until all the blanks have been completed.
3. At your signal, the players will find these words in the word search puzzle and circle them. Words may read across, up, down, or diagonally. The first person to find all the words is the winner.

PUZZLE ANSWERS

1) sinned, died, cross, sins
2) repent, believe, Jesus, Christ, Savior
3) confess, mouth, Lord
4) serve, obey
5) mind, glorify, Father

WORD SEARCH ANSWERS

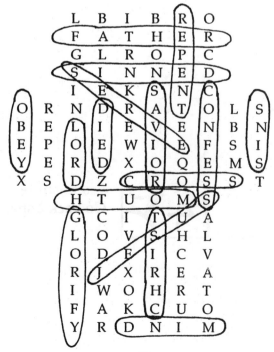

God's Plan of Salvation

1. The Bible says, I have _____ (Romans 3:23) and Jesus

_____ (I Corinthians 15:3). on the _____ (Philippians 2:8) for my

_____ (Galatians 1:4)

2. To be saved, I must _____ of my sin (Luke 13:3) and

_____ on the Lord _____ _____ (Acts

16:31) as my _____ (Acts 5:31).

3. If I am truly saved, I will _____ with my _____ the

_____ Jesus (Romans 10:9-10).

4. After I am saved, I should _____ God (Psalm 100:2) and

_____ Him (Acts 5:29).

5. With my _____ and my mouth, I should _____ God, the

_____ of Jesus Christ (Romans 15:6).

```
              L   B   I   B   R   O
              F   A   T   H   E   R
              G   L   R   O   P   C
              S   I   N   N   E   D
              I   E   K   S   N   C
      O   R   N   D   R   A   T   O   L   S
      B   E   L   I   E   V   E   N   B   N
      E   P   O   E   W   I   E   F   S   I
      Y   E   R   D   X   O   Q   E   M   S
      X   S   D   Z   C   R   O   S   S   T
              H   T   U   O   M   S
              G   C   I   T   U   A
              L   O   V   S   H   L
              O   D   E   I   C   V
              R   J   X   R   E   A
              I   W   O   H   R   T
              F   A   K   C   U   O
              Y   R   D   N   I   M
```

RELAYS & RACES

Spelling Scramble

This game helps children learn to recognize and spell important Bible words.

MEMORY VERSE

"And these words, which I command thee this day, shall be in thine heart." — Deuteronomy 6:6

PREPARATION

Select some Bible words that you would like the children to know from the list below (or make up your own list). With a marker, print each letter of each word on a 3 x 5-inch card, one letter per card. Make enough sets of cards so that each player can have one card. Spell each word with the class, holding up the letters, until the list is learned. You will need a table for this game.

HOW TO PLAY

1. Divide the players into teams, placing as many players on a team as there are letters in the words you are using. Have the teams stand in two lines, facing a table some distance away. Place a set of the letters, scrambled, on the table in front of each team.
2. Say the first word clearly, pause briefly, and then repeat it. At your signal, the first player in each team goes to his set of letters, finds the first letter, and places it near the edge of the table. He

goes back and taps the next player on the hand. That player finds and places the next letter. If a player notices that one of the previous letters is placed incorrectly, he may fix it. The first team to put all letters correctly in place is the winner.
3. To make the game more difficult, after short, single words are learned, use them in combination with other words (such as Holy Bible, Jesus Christ, etc.).

SUGGESTED WORDS

God	Father	heaven	angel
Jesus	hell	Israel	devil
Bible	temple	church	holy
Lord	heart	Christ	believe
Savior	creation	crucify	baptism

Forward-Backward Relay

This game helps children review the names of the books of the Bible.

MEMORY VERSE

"They did not listen or pay attention . . . they went backward and not forward." — Jeremiah 7:24 (NIV)

PREPARATION

With tape or chalk, mark a base line at one end of the room (or outdoors) and a goal line parallel to it, about ten feet away. It will be helpful to have two adult leaders for this game. Bring a pencil and a list of the books of the Bible.

HOW TO PLAY

1. Before playing, review the names of the Bible books. Choose a category of books (the Old or New Testament, major or minor prophets, etc.) for players to name.
2. Have two adult leaders stand behind the goal line. Divide the players into two teams and have them stand in two lines facing the goal line. At your signal, the first player on each team walks rapidly (but does not run) to the goal line, where he will name a book from the chosen category.
3. If he is correct, he turns around, walks back to his team, and taps the hand of the next player. If he says nothing or is incorrect, he must walk backward to his team. The team who finishes first wins.
4. To make the game more difficult, have each team member name a different book. They should call out the book names loudly, and the adult leader should mark them off the list as they are named. No book may be repeated until all have been named.
5. After playing the game, read Jeremiah 7:23-24 and discuss its meaning. Explain that as Christians, we are never standing still. We are moving either forward or backward, as we choose to obey or ignore God's word.

Geography Race

This game helps children recognize important cities, provinces, mountains, and bodies of water in the Holy Land.

MEMORY VERSE

"A land which the Lord thy God careth for: the eyes of the Lord thy God are always upon it." —Deuteronomy 11:12

PREPARATION

Make two photocopies of the map on page 56. Provide a table for the maps or tape them to a wall.

HOW TO PLAY

1. If your pupils are not already familiar with the cities, provinces, mountains, and bodies of water in the Holy Land, show them the map and point out the locations of these places. The first few times you play, it will be helpful to introduce one category at a time.
2. Place both maps on a table or tape them to a wall. Divide the players into two teams, and have them stand one behind the other, in two lines, several feet from the table.
3. Name a place and say, "Go!" The first two players run to their maps and place their finger on the city, mountain, etc. The first player to find the correct place earns 100 points for his team. Continue to play until each team member has played, repeating places in the category, as necessary.
4. As soon as players are familiar with the map locations, play again. This time ask a question from the list below or make up your own. On the word "Go," the players run to their maps, and point to the place where the Bible event happened.

BIBLE EVENT QUESTIONS

1. Where was Jesus born? (Bethlehem) Matthew 2:1
2. Where did Jesus grow up? (Nazareth) Matthew 2:23
3. Where was the temple that Jesus went to as a boy? (Jerusalem) Luke 2:41-49
4. Where was Jesus baptized? (Jordan River) Luke 3:3, 21
5. Where did Jesus perform His first miracle? (Cana) John 2:1-11
6. Did Jesus meet the woman at the well in Galilee, Samaria, or Judea? (Samaria) John 4:1-7
7. In what sea were Peter and Andrew fishing when Jesus called them to follow Him? (Sea of Galilee) Matthew 4:18
8. Into what city did Jesus ride on a colt? (Jerusalem) John 12:12-15
9. On what mount did Jesus pray just before He was captured? (Mount of Olives) Matthew 26:30-36

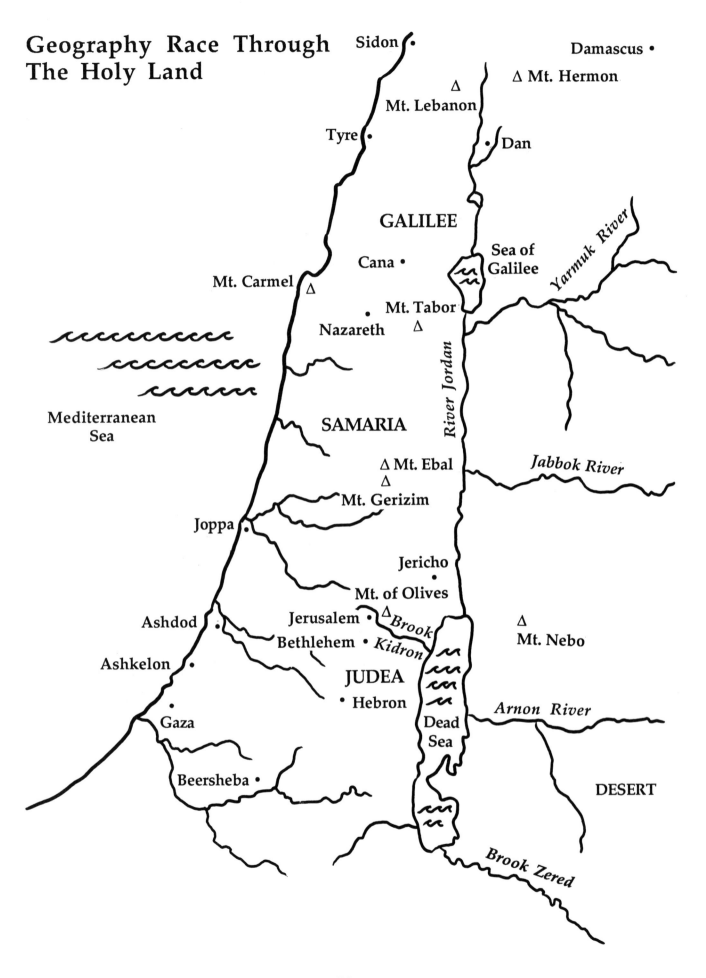

Geography Race Through The Holy Land

Sidon •

Damascus •

△ Mt. Hermon

△ Mt. Lebanon

Tyre •

• Dan

GALILEE

Cana •

Sea of Galilee

Mt. Carmel △

Mt. Tabor

Nazareth • △

Mediterranean Sea

SAMARIA

Yarmuk River

River Jordan

△ Mt. Ebal
△
Mt. Gerizim

Jabbok River

Joppa •

Jericho
•

Mt. of Olives

Ashdod • Jerusalem • △ *Brook*

Bethlehem • *Kidron*

△
Mt. Nebo

Ashkelon •

JUDEA

• Hebron

Gaza •

Dead Sea

Arnon River

Beersheba •

DESERT

Brook Zered

56

Catch and Call

This game helps children remember the names of the books of the Bible and their correct order.

MEMORY VERSE

"My son, do not forget my teaching, but keep my commands in your heart." — Proverbs 3:1 (NIV)

PREPARATION

Plan ahead for this game by asking parents and other adults to collect one gallon plastic water and milk jugs, enough for one jug per child. With a craft knife or scissors, carefully cut off the bottom of each jug, gradually slanting the cut to end just above the handle. (Use sandpaper to smooth any sharp edges, or cover them with tape or felt.) Provide felt pieces, stickers, scissors, markers, and glue for each child. Bring a small rubber ball or tennis ball for the game.

HOW TO PLAY

1. Before playing for the first time, give each player a jug to decorate with stickers and pieces of felt. Have them write their names on the jugs with markers.
2. Divide the players into two teams. Have each team stand side by side in a line, facing the other team. Leave a few feet between the lines. Tell players whether the Bible books will be from the Old or New Testament. Choose a player to begin.
3. The first player calls out the first Bible book, and tosses the ball to the other team. The player who catches it in his jug must name the next book in the correct order and toss the ball back to the other team.

4. Continue until one member misses the ball or cannot name the Bible book. At this point the opposing team gets 100 points and possession of the ball. Continue naming books where the other team stopped. The team with the highest score after all books have been named, wins.

OTHER WAYS TO PLAY

1. Two players may toss the ball back and forth to each other. When a player misses a book or a catch, the other player gets 100 points and resumes the toss, continuing to name the books where the other player stopped. The player with the most points after all books have been named, wins.
2. One player may play at a time, tossing and catching the ball, naming a book each time he catches the ball. When he misses a catch or a book, the next player begins. The player who can name the most books without missing either a catch or a book, wins.

Fish in the Net

This game helps children understand what it means to be fishers of men.

MEMORY VERSE

"Fear not; from henceforth thou shalt catch men."
— Luke 5:10

PREPARATION

Make several copies of the fish pattern below. Provide pencils, crayons or markers (optional), two colors of construction paper, and scissors for the children. Bring a large paper grocery bag and a blindfold. You will need a large open space away from tables and chairs.

HOW TO PLAY

1. Before playing the game for the first time, give each child a pencil and a piece of construction paper (give half the class one color and half the other). Let children share the fish patterns, draw around the pattern, and cut out a fish from construction paper. Some children may draw lines across the paper bag to resemble a fisherman's net.

2. Place the net (the open paper sack) on the floor at one end of the room. Make sure each player has a fish. Divide the players into two teams, according to the color of their fish. Have players stand in two lines, one team facing the other, making a large path to the net. Choose a team to begin. Have the first player stand several feet away from the net. Blindfold him, turn him around two times, and point him toward the net.

3. The player walks toward the net and tries to drop his fish into it. His team members may call out directions to help him reach the net. The opposing team may call misleading directions at the same time, to confuse him. After each player has had a turn, count the number of fish of each color in the net. The team with the most fish in the net wins.

TO TALK ABOUT

Read a story about the miracle of the fishes (Luke 5:1-11 or John 21:6-8). Discuss the story, and ask the children to explain what Jesus meant when he asked us to be fishers of men.

Gifts to the Temple Relay

This game teaches children the importance of giving joyfully.

MEMORY VERSE

"God loveth a cheerful giver."
— II Corinthians 9:7

PREPARATION

Duplicate the circle patterns below. Cut six circles from yellow construction paper for each player. These are "gold coins." (If your group is large, use fewer coins per player.) You will need one plastic or paper drinking straw for each player and two shoe boxes labelled MONEY to represent money chests.

HOW TO PLAY

1. Place the money chests at one end of the room. Divide the children into two teams and have them stand at the other end of the room, in two lines, facing the chests. Give each team member a gold coin and a drinking straw.
2. The first player on each team places one end of his straw in his mouth and the other end on the gold coin. He inhales, holding the coin to the straw with his breath. At your signal, he runs to the money chest, exhales to drop the coin in the chest, and runs back to tap the next player.
3. If a player drops his coin or touches it with his hand, he must pick up the coin with his hand, return to the beginning of his team's line, and try again.
4. When a player has tapped the next in line, he goes to the end of the line and receives another gold coin. Continue until all the coins have been used. The first team with with all their coins in the chest is the winner.

TO TALK ABOUT

Read II Chronicles 24:1-14. The Israelites gave willingly and gladly to the temple that it might be repaired. God asks us to give willingly and joyfully; He loves a cheerful giver. What are some things in addition to money that we can give to the Lord?

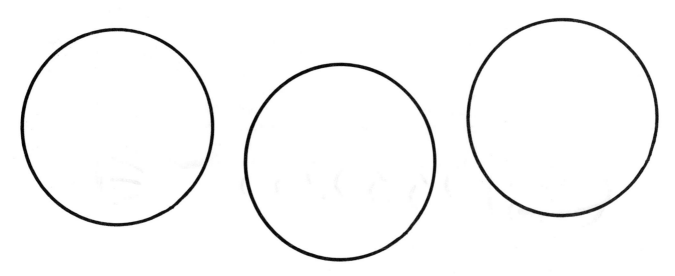

Bible Miracles

1. The Bible tells of two men who went to heaven without dying. Name one of them. (Enoch and Elijah) *Genesis 5:24; II Kings 2:11*
2. Who saw a bush on fire that did not burn up? (Moses) *Exodus 3:1, 2*
3. What dangerous creature did Moses' rod turn into? (snake) *Exodus 4:3*
4. What came out of a rock when Moses struck it with his rod? (water) *Exodus 17:6*
5. What happened to the Israelites' clothing while they wandered in the wilderness for 40 years? (It stayed new.) *Deuteronomy 29:5*
6. What river stopped flowing while the Israelites walked across on dry land? (Jordan) *Joshua 3:17*
7. How many days did Israel march around Jericho before the walls fell down? (seven) *Joshua 6:15*
8. Instead of weapons, what did Gideon and his men use in their battle against the Midianites? (pitchers and lamps) *Judges 7:20*
9. What happened to the sun and the moon when Joshua fought an important battle? (They stood still.) *Joshua 10:13*
10. What creatures brought food to Elijah by a brook? (ravens) *I Kings 17:4*
11. What happened to a leper named Naaman when he dipped in the Jordan River seven times? (He was healed.) *II Kings 5:14*
12. What did Elisha do for a boy who died of sunstroke? (brought him back to life) *II Kings 4:35*
13. What happened to Shadrach, Meshach, and Abednego in the fiery furnace? (They were not burned.) *Daniel 3:27*
14. Who was put in a lion's den and was not hurt? (Daniel) *Daniel 6:22*
15. What was Jesus' first miracle? (turning water into wine) *John 2:9*
16. From how many loaves and fishes did Jesus feed 5000 men? (five loaves, two fishes) *John 6:9*
17. When Jesus cast the demons out of a man, where did He send them? (into pigs) *Luke 8:33*
18. Who was the brother of Martha and Mary whom Jesus raised from the dead? (Lazarus) *John 11:1*
19. What happened to the sun right at noontime when Jesus hung on the cross? (It was darkened.) *Luke 23:45*
20. What greatest miracle of all happened when Jesus had been dead three days? (He came alive.) *Luke 24:6*

True-False Quiz

1. Adam and Eve ate the apples that God told them not to eat. (False — fruit of the tree of knowledge of good and evil) *Genesis 2:17*
2. Abel killed Cain. (False — Cain killed Abel) *Genesis 4:8*
3. Enoch went to heaven without dying. (True) *Genesis 5:24*
4. Moses brought all the animals into the ark. (False — Noah) *Genesis 7:13-15*
5. Abraham lived in a tent in Canaan. (True) *Genesis 12:5-8*
6. Esau and Jacob were twin brothers. (True) *Genesis 25:25-26*
7. Joseph was a slave in Ethiopia. (False—Egypt) *Genesis 37:36*
8. Moses did not go with the Israelites into Canaan. (True) *Deuteronomy 31:2*
9. Saul was the strongest man in the world. (False — Samson) *Judges 14:5-6*
10. David killed a tiger with his bare hands. (False — lion and bear) *I Samuel 17:34-35*
11. Elijah went to heaven without dying. (True) *II Kings 2:11*
12. John the Baptist was Jesus' cousin. (True) *Luke 1:36*
13. Judas denied Jesus three times. (False — betrayed Him) *Matthew 26:14-16*
14. Jesus washed the disciples' hands one night. (False — feet) *John 13:2-12*
15. Stephen was killed for preaching about Jesus by having his head cut off. (False — stoning) *Acts 7:58*
16. At the first of his life, Paul's name was Saul. (True) *Acts 13:9*
17. Saul (Paul) was saved when God spoke to him in the middle of the night. (False — at noonday) *Acts 22:6*
18. When Peter was put in prison, a Christian soldier came and took him out. (False — an angel) *Acts 12:5-10*
19. When Paul and Silas were in prison, all the doors were opened by a great flood. (False — earthquake) *Acts 16:25-26*
20. Only people whose names are written in the Lamb's Book of Life may enter heaven. (True) *Revelation 21:27*
21. The heavenly city won't have a sun or a moon for light. (True) *Revelation 21:23*
22. The heavenly city will have twelve gates made of diamonds. (False—pearls) *Revelation 21:21*

Things in the Bible Which Were Thrown

1. What did David throw at Goliath? (A stone) *I Samuel 17:49*
2. Where was Daniel thrown for praying to God? (Lions' den) *Daniel 6:16*
3. When Moses threw his rod on the ground, what did it become? (A serpent) *Exodus 7:9*
4. While David was playing his harp, what did King Saul throw at him? (A javelin or spear) *I Samuel 18:11*
5. What were Peter and Andrew throwing into the sea when Jesus called them to follow Him? (Nets) *Matthew 4:18*
6. What man did sailors throw out of a ship in a bad storm? (Jonah) *Jonah 1:15*
7. What were Paul and Silas thrown into for preaching about Jesus? (Prison) *Acts 16:23*
8. Where should we throw all our cares and troubles? (Upon God) *I Peter 5:7*
9. What did Aaron and the Egyptian magicians throw down that turned into serpents? (Rods)

Exodus 7:10-12

10. Where were Shadrach, Meshach, and Abednego thrown for not bowing down to an idol? (Fiery furnace) *Daniel 3:20*
11. When Peter threw a hook into the sea, what was in the mouth of the fish that he caught? (A coin) *Matthew 17:27*

Who Was I?

1. I was a woman who was never born. Was I <u>Eve</u> or Mary? *Genesis 2:22*
2. I was the first son of Adam and Eve. Was I Abel or <u>Cain</u>? *Genesis 4:1*
3. I was a slave who became a ruler in Egypt. Was I Judah or <u>Joseph</u>? *Genesis 41:41*
4. I received the Ten Commandments from God. Was I <u>Moses</u> or Noah? *Exodus 31:18*
5. I suffered from boils. Was I Jonah or <u>Job</u>? *Job 2:7*
6. I was turned into a pillar of salt. Was I Sarah or <u>Lot's wife</u>? *Genesis 19:26*
7. I was the first king of Israel. Was I <u>Saul</u> or David? *I Samuel 10:21-24*
8. I was the queen who kept the Jews from being killed. Was I <u>Esther</u> or Ruth? *Esther 7:3*
9. I heard a donkey talk. Was I <u>Balaam</u> or Boaz? *Numbers 22:28*
10. I saw a hand, writing on a wall. Was I Pharaoh or <u>Belshazzar</u>? *Daniel 5:5, 9*
11. I was the mother of John the Baptist. Was I <u>Elisabeth</u> or Martha? *Luke 1:57, 60*

Fishing Quiz

1. On what day of creation did God make fish? (Fifth) *Genesis 1:21, 23*
2. Whom did God put in charge of all the fish? (Adam) *Genesis 1:28*
3. Why did God prepare a fish to swallow Jonah? (Because Jonah wouldn't go to Ninevah and preach.) *Jonah 1:2, 3, 10*
4. How long was Jonah in the fish's stomach? (Three days and nights) *Matthew 12:40*
5. What did Jonah do in the fish's stomach? (He prayed.) *Jonah 2:1*
6. What four disciples were fishermen before they followed Jesus? (Peter, Andrew, James, John) *Matthew 4:18, 21*
7. What did Jesus tell Peter, Andrew, James, and John that He wanted them to fish for? (Men) *Luke 5:10*
8. How many fish did the little boy give Jesus? (Two) *John 6:9*
9. How many men did Jesus feed with the boy's five loaves and two fish? (5000) *John 6:10*
10. What did Jesus tell the disciples to do when they had fished all night and caught nothing? (Let down their nets) *John 21:16*

What The Bible Says About Money

1. For how many pieces of silver was Joseph sold — 10 or 20? (20) *Genesis 37:28*
2. Where did Joseph put his brothers' money when they bought grain in Egypt — in their sacks or their hands? (Sacks) *Genesis 42:25*
3. How much was a tithe in the Old Testament — five or ten percent? (10) *Leviticus 27:32*
4. When people brought money to help Joash repair the temple, what did they put it in — a chest or a bucket? (Chest) *II Kings 12:9*
5. How did God say people had robbed Him — by stealing things from the temple or by not paying tithes? (Tithes) *Malachi 3:8*
6. Which did David say was better to him than thousands of gold and silver pieces — God's law or good health? (God's law) *Psalm 119:72*
7. When Jesus' disciples went out to preach, what did Jesus tell them about money — take plenty or take none? (None) *Luke 9:3*
8. Why did the rich young ruler turn away from Jesus — because he loved money or he loved his wife? (Money) *Luke 18:22-23*
9. What did Solomon ask God for instead of riches and honor — long life or wisdom? (Wisdom) *I Kings 3:9-12*

Where Did It Happen?

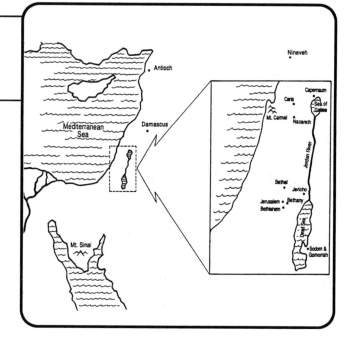

1. Where did the first sin take place? (Garden of Eden) *Genesis 2:8; 3:1-7*
2. Where were Noah and his family during the flood? (In the ark) *Genesis 7:7*
3. Where did God cause people to speak in different languages? (Tower of Babel) *Genesis 11:9*
4. Where did Abram go when God told him to leave his own country? (Canaan or the Promised Land) *Genesis 12:1-5*
5. Where did God rain down fire and brimstone? (Sodom and Gomorrah) *Genesis 19:24*
6. Where was Joseph sold as a slave? (Egypt) *Genesis 37:28*
7. Where were the Israelites when Pharaoh chased them, and God held back the water for them to pass over? (Red Sea) *Exodus 13:18, 14:21-22*
8. Where did God provide food and water for the Israelites by a miracle? (The wilderness) *Exodus 16:1-16; 17:5-7*
9. Where did Moses receive the Ten Commandments? (Mount Sinai) *Exodus 19:18; 20:1*
10. Where did the walls fall down when the Israelites marched around them? (Jericho) *Joshua 6:1, 20*
11. Where was Jonah for three days when the sailors threw him into the sea? (Inside a great fish) *Jonah 1:17; 2:10*
12. Where was Jesus born? (Bethlehem) *Matthew 2:1*
13. Where was the temple that Jesus went to at the age of 12? (Jerusalem) *Luke 2:41-42*

14. Where was Jesus baptized? (Jordan River) *Mark 1:9*
15. Where did Jesus live until He was 30 years old? (Nazareth) *Matthew 2:23*
16. Where did Jesus walk on the water? (Sea of Galilee) *Matthew 14:25*
17. Where did Peter find money to pay taxes for himself and Jesus? (In a fish's mouth) *Matthew 17:27*
18. Where was Jesus crucified? (Calvary or Golgotha) *Matthew 27:33*
19. Where were Jesus and the disciples when Jesus ascended back to heaven? (Mount of Olives) *Acts 1:12*
20. Where will believers meet Jesus when He comes back to take us to heaven? (In the air) *I Thessalonians 4:17*